POPULAR HITS

T0085224

HOW TO USE THE CD ACCOMPANIMENT:

A MELODY CUE APPEARS ON THE RIGHT CHANNEL ONLY. IF YOUR CD PLAYER HAS A BALANCE ADJUSTMENT, YOU CAN ADJUST THE VOLUME OF THE MELODY BY TURNING DOWN THE RIGHT CHANNEL.

THE CD IS PLAYABLE ON ANY CD PLAYER, AND IS ALSO ENHANCED SO MAC AND PC USERS CAN ADJUST THE RECORDING TO ANY TEMPO WITHOUT CHANGING THE PITCH!

ISBN 978-1-61774-001-5

HAL•LEONARD®
CORPORATION
7777 W. BLUEMOUND RD. P.O. BOX 13819 MILWAUKEE, WI 53213

Visit Hal Leonard Online at
www.halleonard.com

◆1 BREAKEVEN

Horn

Words and Music by STEPHEN KIPNER, ANDREW FRAMPTON, DANIEL O'DONOGHUE and MARK SHEEHAN

❷ THE CLIMB

from HANNAH MONTANA: THE MOVIE

HORN

Words and Music by
JESSI ALEXANDER and JON MABE

❸FALLIN' FOR YOU

Horn

Words and Music by
COLBIE CAILLAT and RICK NOWELS

FIREFLIES

HORN

Words and Music by
ADAM YOUNG

⬥ HALO

Horn

Moderately

Words and Music by BEYONCÉ KNOWLES,
RYAN TEDDER and EVAN BOGART

◆HEY, SOUL SISTER

Horn

Words and Music by PAT MONAHAN, ESPEN LIND and AMUND BJORKLAND

♦ I GOTTA FEELING

Words and Music by WILL ADAMS,
ALLAN PINEDA, JAIME GOMEZ, STACY FERGUSON,
DAVID GUETTA and FREDERIC RIESTERER

Horn

8 I'M YOURS

HORN

Words and Music by
JASON MRAZ

◆⑨ LOVE STORY

HORN

Words and Music by
TAYLOR SWIFT

15

small notes optional

NEED YOU NOW

Horn

Words and Music by HILLARY SCOTT,
CHARLES KELLEY, DAVE HAYWOOD and JOSH KEAR

POKER FACE

Words and Music by
STEFANI GERMANOTTA and REDONE

Horn

◆ SMILE

Horn

Words and Music by BLAIR DALY, JEREMY BOSE, MATTHEW SHAFER and JOHN HARDING

VIVA LA VIDA

Horn

Words and Music by GUY BERRYMAN,
JON BUCKLAND, WILL CHAMPION and CHRIS MARTIN

14 YOU BELONG WITH ME

Horn

Words and Music by
TAYLOR SWIFT and LIZ ROSE

USE SOMEBODY

HORN

Words and Music by CALEB FOLLOWILL, NATHAN FOLLOWILL,
JARED FOLLOWILL and MATTHEW FOLLOWILL